12 EDUCATORS WHO CHANGED THE WORLD

by Vicki C. Hayes

12

STORY LIBRARY

MORE TO EXPLORE

www.12StoryLibrary.com

12-Story Library is an imprint of Bookstaves.

Photographs ©: PD, cover, 1; PD, 4; KJJS/CC2.0, 5; Ehirsh/PD, 6; Sajaganesandip/CC4.0, 7; Bancroft1883/YouTube, 8; PD, 9; Harris & Ewing/PD, 10; Frances Benjamin Johnston/PD, 11; Chawla.nishant/CC3.0, 12; PD, 13; Center for Public Leadership & Tom Fitzsimmons/CC2.0, 14; Jim.henderson/CC1.0. 15; Lola García-Ajofrín/Getty Images, 16; vectorfusionart/Shutterstock.com, 17; Kettering Foundation/YouTube, 18; Robert L. Knudsen/PD, 19; Sebastian Derungs/World Economic Forum/CC2.0, 20; Meghan - Collab KA/CC2.0, 21; C.W. Bardeen/PD, 22; Johannes Ronge/Internet Archive Book Images/CC, 23; Kippelboy/CC3.0, 23; G. Gershoff/Getty Images, 24; Boyd Matson/YouTube, 25; CSU Archives/Alamy, 26; Joshua Seong/Verywell/PD, 27; Edmond Joaillier/PD, 28; Neil Grabowsky/Montclair Film Festival/CC2.0, 29

ISBN
9781632357168 (hardcover)
9781632358257 (paperback)
9781645820048 (ebook)

Library of Congress Control Number: 2019938650

Printed in the United States of America
July 2019

About the Cover

Maria Montessori in an undated photo.

Access free, up-to-date content on this topic plus a full digital version of this book. Scan the QR code on page 31 or use your school's login at 12StoryLibrary.com.

Table of Contents

1

Maria Montessori: Giving Children Independence

Maria Montessori was an Italian educator, doctor, and scientist. She was born in a small town in Italy in 1870. In 1875, her family moved to Rome. In 1890, she became one of the first women in Italy to go to medical school. By 1896, she was a doctor.

5,000+

Number of Montessori schools in the United States

- Montessori schools teach children from infancy to age 18.
- Children focus on the process of play, not the end result.
- Children are encouraged to use all their senses in hands-on learning.

Maria Montessori in 1913.

In 1906, Montessori was asked to create a child-care center for poor, inner-city children in Rome. These were children people thought were unable to learn. Montessori called her center Casa dei Bambini, or Children's House. She let children choose the activities they wanted to explore and work at their own pace.

Montessori thought these experiences would make children want to learn. She was right. The children played with the materials in the classroom. They made discoveries. They worked calmly and peacefully. They were polite and kind to each other and took care of their surroundings. They were able to concentrate, and they learned. Casa dei Bambini was a success.

Montessori thought independent learning was important. She created activities children could do on their own. These activities also helped children learn to fix their own mistakes. Montessori schools became very popular. Today there are over 20,000 Montessori schools worldwide.

PEACE AND JUSTICE

Peace and social justice are important in Montessori education. Maria Montessori lived through two World Wars. Her own experience convinced her that peace and social justice needed to be part of her schools. She wanted children to learn to respect their friends and their work space. The idea of peace exists all through the Montessori curriculum.

A Montessori classroom in Indiana in 2012.

2

Howard Gardner: Many Ways to Be Smart

Howard Gardner in 2010.

Howard Gardner is a psychologist and a professor at Harvard University. He was born in 1943 in Scranton, Pennsylvania. His parents were Jewish refugees from Nazi Germany.

Gardner studies how people learn. In 1983, after years of research, he proposed a new idea about learning. He called it the Theory of Multiple Intelligences. Gardner had concluded there is not just one way to be smart. People have different kinds of minds. They learn and remember in different ways. This means they can be smart in different ways. People can be smart with words or numbers, music, or how they perceive things. They can be smart with how they move their bodies. They can be smart about the natural world. They can be smart with how they understand other people or themselves.

Gardner's ideas gave teachers new ways to see their students. Because children don't all learn in the same way, they shouldn't all be taught in the same way. Many schools changed their programs and teaching methods. They trained teachers differently. Students learned to appreciate their own ways of being smart. Today schools, businesses, and organizations around the world use Gardner's theory.

7

Number of intelligences Gardner first suggested

- Later he added an eighth intelligence for people good at understanding nature.
- He thinks there may be even more intelligences.
- Gardner is one of the world's leading thinkers.

THINK ABOUT IT

Howard Gardner came up with eight ways people can be smart. What is your strongest way to be smart? Why do you think that? Are you smart in more than one way?

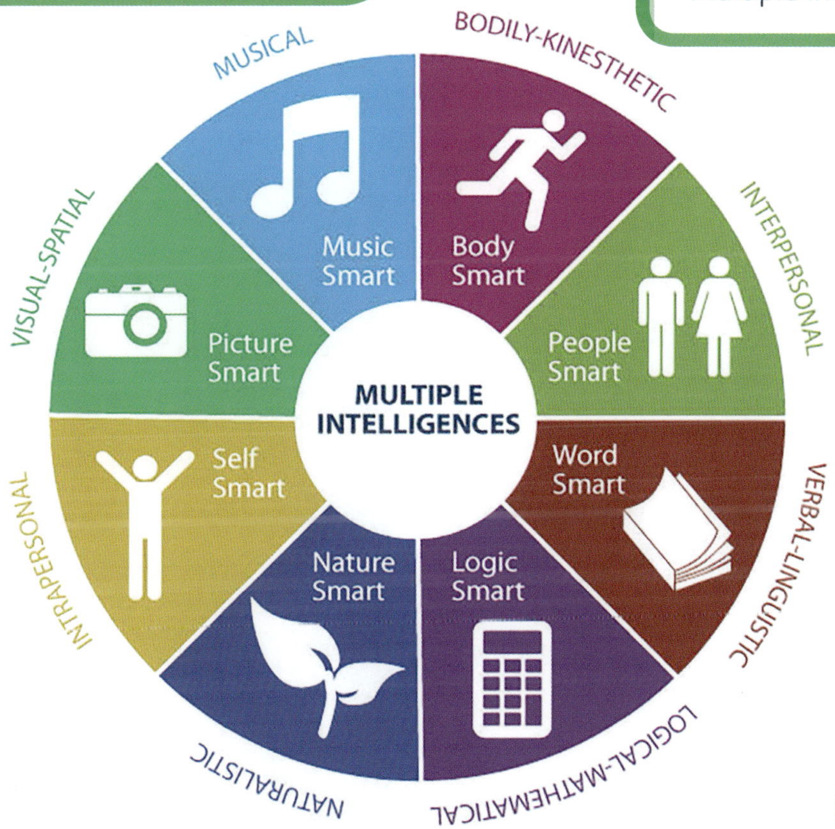

Gardner's Theory of Multiple Intelligences.

3

Margaret Bancroft: Every Child Deserves to Learn

Margaret Bancroft was a schoolteacher from Philadelphia. She was born there in 1854. In the 1800s, children with mental or physical problems did not go to school. They were put in institutions. No one even tried to teach them. Bancroft felt these children could learn. She believed they had a right to be educated. In 1883, she rented a small house in New Jersey and started her own school. She was only 29 years old. The school was for children with special needs.

Bancroft said children with special needs required special programs. She created individualized programs for each child. Then she taught teachers how to work with the children. She made sure the children had exercise and nutritious food. The children went on trips to museums, concerts, and the circus. Bancroft's work got doctors to pay attention to these children. Doctors realized they needed to help them, not just send them to institutions.

Bancroft's work started people thinking about special education. Today children in the United States

Statue of Bancroft in Haddonfield, NJ.

with special needs have the right to a free public education. There are many programs for them. There are also programs for training teachers.

The original Bancroft school has grown into a large organization. It helps people of all ages and many different challenges to lead happy, fulfilled lives.

1

Number of students who attended Margaret Bancroft's school in the first year

- Today Bancroft helps 2,000 people every year.
- It has 2,500 employees with many different skills.
- It has 14 locations in 3 states and 200 group homes.

4 Booker T. Washington: Helping African Americans Succeed

Booker T. Washington was born into slavery in Virginia in 1856. After the Civil War, his family moved to West Virginia. He put himself through school and became a teacher. In 1881, he was asked to head a new school for African Americans. Today it is called Tuskegee University. Washington was its first president.

At the beginning, Tuskegee had one room and 30 students. Its goal was to train African Americans to be farmers. It was hard because Tuskegee had no money. Many white people did not want black people to be educated. Washington traveled all over the country raising money for the school. Most of the money came from white people. Sometimes he had to promise the white people that his school would not be better than white schools.

Booker T. Washington in 1905.

Washington put a lot of his ideas into Tuskegee. He taught African American students that economic progress would take time. He said they had to work hard and be patient. Then they would be accepted as citizens in society. Washington believed

RIVALRY WITH W.E.B. DU BOIS

W.E.B. Du Bois and Booker T. Washington were two important black Americans. They both wanted equality. But they had different ideas of how to get it. Washington said black Americans should study, work hard, and be patient. DuBois said they should demand their rights and fight for equality. Their argument set the stage for the modern civil rights movement.

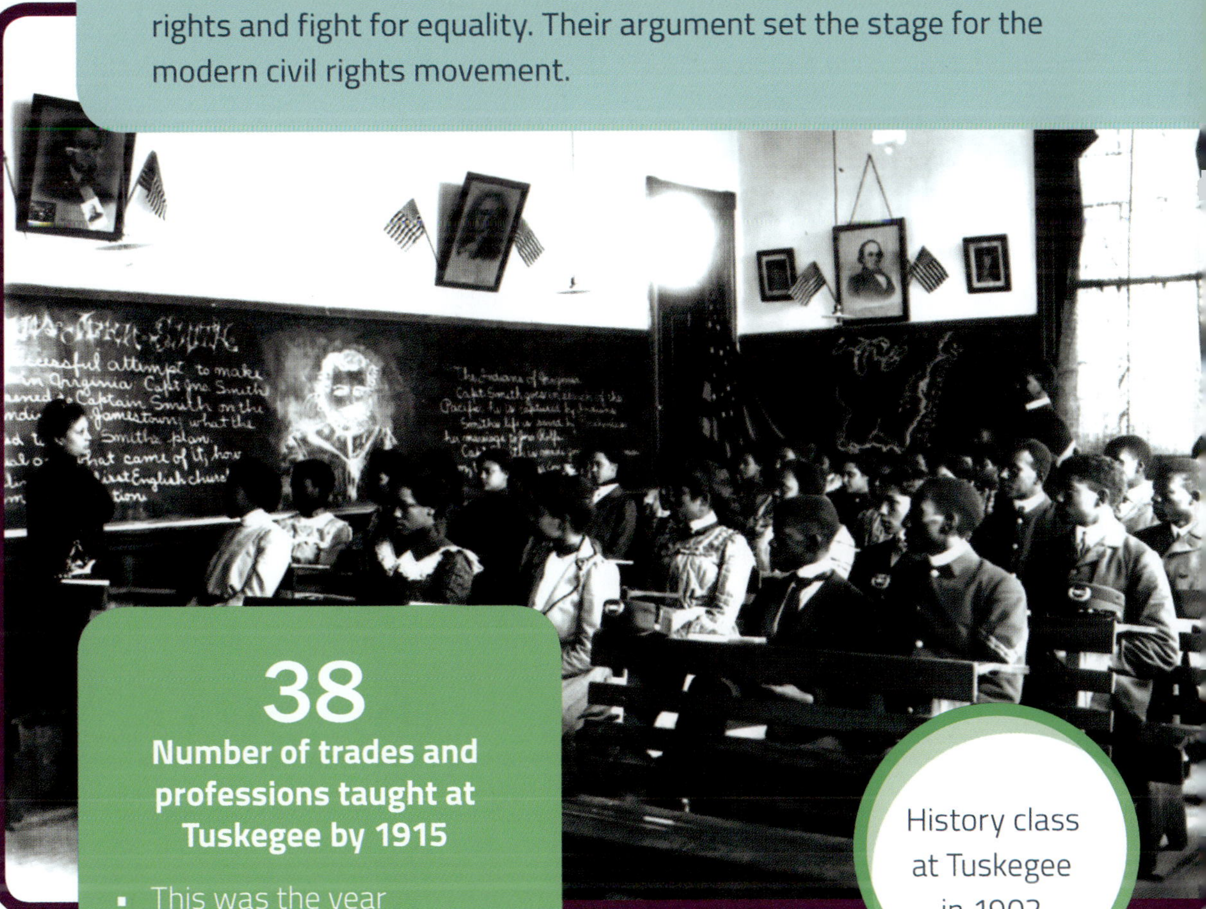

History class at Tuskegee in 1902.

38

Number of trades and professions taught at Tuskegee by 1915

- This was the year Booker T. Washington died.
- By then, Tuskegee had more than 100 buildings.
- It had 1,500 students, over 200 teachers, and an endowment of almost $2 million.

the best way to help black people was to give them skills. He worked hard to make his school a success.

5

Savitribai Phule: Fighting for Girls in India

Savitribai Phule was the first female teacher in India. She was born in a small village in 1831. At the time, child marriage was legal in India. Savitribai was married at age 9 to 12-year-old Jyotirao Phule. He taught her to read and write.

When Phule was in her teens, she and her husband started a school. It was the first Indian-run school for girls. In 1848, she became a teacher. This made many people angry. In 1852, the British government named her Best Teacher. Phule and her husband opened more schools for girls and women.

In India, people are separated into castes. Certain castes

A bust of Savitribai Phule in Pune, India.

18

Number of schools opened by Savitribai Phule and her husband

- Many people were angry that Phule taught women and lower-caste children.
- They threw cow dung, mud, and stones at her when she walked to school.
- She always carried two saris so she could change her clothes.

are higher than others. People in the lower castes are not treated well. Phule fought for all people to be treated equally. She opened shelters for poor women, widows, and child brides. She started schools for children from lower castes and fought against child marriage.

In 1897, the bubonic plague appeared in India. Phule opened a clinic. While caring for a sick child, she caught the disease and died. Phule is remembered today as a feminist and social reformer.

A page from the manuscript *Seventy-two Specimens of Castes in India* from 1837 confirms the perceptions of the time.

THE CASTE SYSTEM

In India, people were divided into four main castes. The two highest castes were Brahmins (priests and teachers) and Kshatriyas (warriors and rulers). Below them were Vaishyas (farmers, traders, and merchants) and Shudras (laborers). There were also the Dalits, or untouchables (street sweepers and latrine cleaners). People from different castes did not mix. They could not live together or marry. The bottom castes had the worst jobs and were mistreated by others. Today castes are outlawed. But the caste system still exists.

6

Geoffrey Canada: Rebuilding Communities Block by Block

Geoffrey Canada in 2011.

Geoffrey Canada is an educator, activist, and author. Born in 1952, he grew up in a poor, sometimes violent neighborhood in the South Bronx in New York City. His mother struggled to raise him and his three brothers on her own. She also taught him the value of education. Canada graduated from college and got a master's degree in education from Harvard University. He decided to work with kids in poor neighborhoods.

Canada went back to New York City. In 1983, he got a job in Harlem. He worked for an organization that became the Harlem Children's Zone (HCZ). He was its leader from 1990 to 2014. HCZ helps children from low-income families. It funds and operates programs, schools, and social services for kids and parents. It supports kids from birth through college. It works to heal whole communities from the disease of poverty.

HCZ started by helping people on one block. It grew to 24 blocks, then 60 blocks, then 97 blocks. Today it is a model of this type of work for the world.

Canada made sure people knew about HCZ. He appeared on popular

Harlem Children's Zone and Promise Academy in New York.

27,537

Children and adults served by Harlem Children's Zone in 2017

- Harlem Children's Zone offers parenting workshops and preschool programs.
- It teaches children healthy habits to fight obesity.
- It has run workshops in 477 US communities and 161 international communities.

TV shows like *60 Minutes, Oprah,* and *Anderson Cooper 360°*. Many articles were written about Canada and HCZ. In 2011, *TIME* magazine named him one of the 100 most influential people in the world. In 2014, *Fortune* named him one of the 50 greatest leaders in the world.

7

Phalla Neang: Changing Life for Students Who Are Blind

Phalla Neang in 2017.

Phalla Neang is a Cambodian teacher. She was born in Phnom Penh in 1960. She teaches students who are blind or cannot see well. Her first job was for the United Nations in 1986. She worked in Thailand, teaching students at a refugee camp. In 1991, she returned to Cambodia. She began working for Krousar Thmey. This was the first Cambodian aid foundation for underprivileged children. In 1994, Krousar Thmey opened a school for students with vision problems. Neang was one of their teachers.

Neang used Braille with her students. She was the first teacher of Braille in Cambodia. Khmer is the official language of Cambodia. Neang created a Khmer version of Braille. She also had new ideas about teaching blind students. She knew these students were often very good at music. They were also good at learning foreign languages. Neang made music a big part of her teaching. She taught the children English and computer skills.

Many Cambodians thought that people with blindness couldn't learn. They believed these people had done something wrong in a past life that made them blind. They would not talk to them. Neang worked to change the way people thought. She wanted to show that blind people are not so different.

8

Students who attended the new school for the blind in the first year

- Parents in Cambodia often hid their blind children by keeping them at home.
- Phalla Neang had to visit homes to find these children.
- Krousar Thmey now runs five schools with 350 blind students and 174 workers.

KHMER BRAILLE

Braille is a form of written language. It is read through touch. Letters are made with raised dots. Students read the words by feeling the dots with their fingers. Braille works well with many languages. But the Khmer language uses grammar differently. It is more complicated. Neang had to invent Khmer Braille.

8

Edmund Gordon: Giving Poor Children a Head Start

Edmund Gordon in 2011.

Edmund Gordon is an African American psychologist and professor at Yale University. Born in North Carolina in 1921, he has helped society in many areas. One thing he did was to help children at risk. These are children who are less likely than others to succeed in school and life.

In 1965, Gordon was asked to work on a new program for the US government. It was called Head Start. Gordon became a founder and designer of Head Start. Its goal was to help poor children catch up to their peers before starting school. It also made families and communities stronger. Head Start continues today. It helps children at risk under five. It works to make child-care programs better and early education programs stronger. It gives families information on nutritious food and health care.

Gordon did other work in education. He noticed there was a gap between many students of color and white students. This gap was most obvious in test scores. Gordon called it an "achievement gap." He has said the United States needs to

Lady Bird Johnson, former First Lady, visits a Head Start classroom in 1966.

work harder to close this gap. Today Gordon writes books and gives talks. He keeps helping students of color who live in low-income and working-class communities.

50+

Number of years Head Start has been around

- Since 1965, Head Start has helped 32 million children.
- It currently serves more than one million children and their families each year.
- Young children are given a love for learning that helps them achieve in life.

THINK ABOUT IT

There are many reasons for the achievement gap. These include poverty, failing schools, racism, and poor health. They include growing up in a household where no one speaks English. Can you think of more reasons for the gap?

9

Wendy Kopp: Teaching for the World

Wendy Kopp was born in Texas in 1967. She grew up in Austin, San Antonio, and Dallas. She went to good schools and was an outstanding student. Then she went to Princeton University in New Jersey. She noticed something about some of the new friends she made there.

489

Number of Teach for America corps members in 1990, the first year

- Teach for America began in six communities.
- Today it has 60,000 members and alumni working in 51 regions.
- Teach for All works in 49 countries on 6 continents.

They were not as ready for college as she was. She found out they had gone to poor schools. She realized schools in the United States were not equal.

Kopp wanted to help. She came up with a new concept called Teach for America. Top college graduates would teach in poor public schools. They would teach for two years. This would help the students and would also be a service to the country.

Kopp spent a lot of time raising money for her program. Many people liked the idea and wanted to contribute. When Kopp had raised $2.5 million, she started Teach for America. The first year was very successful, and the program grew from there. Kopp was its leader for 24 years. Today about 7,000 Teach for America corps members are working in schools across the United States.

Meanwhile, people in other countries learned about the Teach for America model. They wanted to use it in their countries, too. In 2007, Kopp co-founded Teach for All. This organization works around the world. It is made of many different groups. They work to give children everywhere a stronger education. Teach for All helps improve schools. It gives people better opportunities and works to get rid of unfairness.

Teach for America corps members work in schools arcross the US.

10

Friedrich Froebel: The Father of Kindergarten

A lithograph of Friedrich Froebel from 1896.

Born in 1782, Friedrich Froebel was a German educator. As a young man, he studied forestry. Then he became a teacher. In 1816, Froebel opened a school with friends. It was very successful. He trained elementary school teachers and started teaching very young children. He saw how important the early years were for children.

In 1837, Froebel opened his own school. He called it Kindergarten, or Garden of Children. His kindergarten had singing and dancing, gardening, and play. Froebel liked watching young children play. He saw that children learn through play. They use play to understand the world. Froebel was one of the first educators to recognize this.

Froebel wanted his students to create things. He gave them materials for their play like sticks, clay, sand, chalk, stones, and paper. He studied how children used these materials. Froebel wrote books about play. Because of him, many educators changed the way they thought about children's play. People in other countries started kindergartens. Froebel's ideas were very popular in the United States.

FROEBEL AND FRANK LLOYD WRIGHT

Frank Lloyd Wright has been called America's greatest architect. He was born in 1867. By then, the Froebel play sets were known around the world. When Wright was nine years old, his mother saw them in Philadelphia. She bought a set of blocks. Wright played with them for years. They had a strong influence on his architecture. He was still talking about the blocks when he was 88 years old.

A guide for Froebel's system for infant training from 1858, and a reproduction of one of his play sets.

10

Number of play sets Friedrich Froebel designed

- Froebel called his play sets Gifts. They were the first educational toys.
- The first Gift included squishy, colorful yarn balls.
- Other Gifts had wood spheres, cylinders, prisms, and blocks. Some had sticks and rings.

11

Kakenya Ntaiya: Empowering Girls in Kenya

Kakenya Ntaiya was born in Kenya in 1978. A member of the Maasai people of East Africa, she grew up in the traditional way. She was engaged to be married at five. She was expected to marry at 15 and start a family. But she talked her father into letting her finish high school. Then she wanted to go to college. She told her village that if they let her go, she would come back later and help them. Her village raised money to pay for her flight. Ntaiya went to a school in the United States. She was the first girl from her village to do so.

Ntaiya became the first youth advisor to the United Nations. She traveled around the world, talking about girls' education. Then she went back to the United States. She got a PhD in education. Finally, she returned to Kenya like she promised.

In 2008, Ntaiya started an organization called Kakenya's Dream. The goal is to educate girls. Kakenya's Dream empowers and motivates girls. Then the girls can change their families, their communities, and their lives. So

17
Percentage of girls in rural Kenya who finish primary school

- The Kakenya Center's boarding school started with 30 girls in 2009.
- So far, it has provided safe schooling for more than 350 girls.
- 100 percent of the center's girls finish school.

THINK ABOUT IT

Many cultures once thought the education of boys and girls should be different. Some still do. Some cultures thought girls should not be educated at all. Why do you think they had this idea?

far, the organization's three programs have served over 8,000 girls. In 2009, Ntaiya opened the Kakenya Center for Excellence. It is a boarding school just for girls that offers art and science. It has been growing every year.

Ntaiya at her boarding school for Maasai girls in rural Kenya in 2018.

12

Jean Piaget: Understanding How a Child's Mind Works

Jean Piaget in 1974.

Born in Switzerland in 1896, Jean Piaget was a biologist and a psychologist. At first, he was mainly interested in mollusks. Then he got interested in psychology.

Piaget was especially curious about how children learn. He wanted to know how their minds work. Up until then, children were viewed as miniature adults. They just weren't as smart as adults. Piaget learned about children by watching them play. He asked them questions and listened to their answers. Piaget realized that children think in very different ways from adults.

To explain how children think, Piaget came up with the Theory of Cognitive Development. This is a way to describe how thinking changes with age and experience. He described four stages every child goes through on the way to adulthood. Piaget believed that children learn best by doing and exploring. He thought trial-and-error should be part of learning. He said children can't learn new information if they aren't ready.

Piaget's theory helped teachers rethink how they were teaching. Many schools today use Piaget's ideas. Doctors use his stages to see if children are developing normally.

OBJECT PERMANENCE

Piaget did a lot of tests with infants. For one test, he covered a toy with a blanket. Some infants promptly forgot about the toy. For them, it no longer existed. Other infants reached for the toy. They knew it was still there. The ability to understand that a hidden object still exists is called "object permanence." It usually happens around eight or nine months of age. This is during Piaget's first stage of cognitive development.

1929

Year when Jean Piaget became Director of the International Bureau of Education in Geneva, Switzerland

- Piaget was a big believer in education.
- He thought education was the main challenge facing all peoples.
- He said education was the only thing that could save our societies from collapse.

Piaget's Stages of Cognitive Development

Sensorimotor Stage	Preoperational Stage	Concrete Operational Stage	Formal Operational Stage
Birth to 2 yrs	2 to 7 yrs	7 to 11 yrs	12 and up

verywell

More Educators Who Changed the World

Aristotle

Aristotle (384–322 BCE) lived over 2,000 years ago. He was a Greek philosopher and scientist. He started a school in Athens, Greece, called the Lyceum. Aristotle taught students to use reasoning and logic. He believed questioning was important. He believed in learning for learning's sake. And he believed strongly in public education.

Nadia Boulanger

Nadia Boulanger (1887–1979) was a French composer and conductor. She was the first woman to conduct several well-known orchestras. She was also a music teacher. Many of her students became famous composers. These included Virgil Thomson, Thea Musgrave, and Aaron Copland.

Nadia Boulanger in 1925.

Bill Nye

At first, Bill Nye (1955–) was a mechanical engineer. Then he became a science educator and a TV presenter known as Bill Nye, the Science Guy. He hosted a fast-paced TV show that taught science. It was aimed at pre-teens. It used quirky humor and unusual experiments. The show was very popular.

Bill Nye in 2017.

Lucy Sprague Mitchell

Lucy Sprague Mitchell (1878–1967) started Bank Street College of Education in 1916 in New York City. Bank Street is a teachers' college. Mitchell said schools must teach the "whole child." Her college trains the "whole teacher." Bank Street has a children's school where teachers can practice their skills.

Glossary

caste
A social class of people in India that is given or denied privileges.

conflict resolution
A way for people to find a peaceful ending to a fight or argument.

curriculum
The courses taught by a school.

economic
Having to do with money.

endowment
Money given to support a college, university, library, or other organization.

individualized
Made or changed to fit a person's needs.

obesity
Being very fat or overweight.

peers
People of the same status or belonging to the same group.

permanence
Lasting or staying unchanged.

psychologist
A person who studies the human mind.

refugee
A person forced to leave their country because of terrible conditions.

sari
A long piece of cloth draped around the body and worn by women in some Asian countries.

theory
An idea that explains something.

Read More

Boyce, Jo Ann Allen and Debbie Levy. *This Promise of Change: One Girl's Story in the Fight for School Equality.* New York: Bloomsbury Children's Books, 2019.

Buckley, James Jr. *Who Was Booker T. Washington?* New York: Penguin Workshop, 2018.

Schwartz, Heather. *Science Educator and Advocate Bill Nye.* Stem Trailblazer Biographies. Minneapolis, MN: Lerner Publishing Group, 2018.

Stevenson, Robin. *Kid Activists: True Tales of Childhood from Champions of Change.* Philadelphia, PA: Quirk Books, 2019.

Index

About the Author

Vicki C. Hayes has a master's degree in early childhood education and over 30 years of experience teaching children of all ages. She currently works as a teacher and writer.